1

The First People ate fruit, nuts and seeds from many plants. The First People were able to pick safe food. Some forms of fungi were eaten by the First People. WARNING! Do not eat any wild foods! These foods are UNSAFE!

3

Reeds in water were used for food. The First People ate the root of the reeds. It contained gooey food like bread.

5

Water plants provided food for the First People. The stalks of the water plants were eaten.

7

This was called the bush nut. It was a forest tree eaten by the First People. It is now called the Macadamia, *mac-ad-am-ia*. This nut is sold all over the world.

9

This nut comes from a pine tree. It is the bunya pine. It grows in the mountains in Queensland. It was a very popular food for the First People.

11

This fruit comes from a small bush in the rainforests. It is called the finger lime. It is a very popular food today. The First People would have eaten this fruit.

Wattle trees grow all over Australia. There are many types of wattle trees. The seeds from the wattle are crushed. The crushed seeds are made into flour and cooked. This made a very good food for the First People.

15

These small fruits were called Lilly Pillies. These fruits came from forest trees. The fruit was eaten by the Aboriginal people of Australia.

17

The forests and grasslands had food for the First People. It was not the food we use now. The fruits and foods were different. The foods were good and allowed the First People to be strong and healthy.

19

Foods could be found in all parts of Australia. Aboriginal people knew when to eat the foods. The First People knew how to make the food. It was important to know what to do with the food so that it did not make you sick.

21

Desert grass seeds were taken and crushed. The seeds would make flour. The flour would be mixed with water and cooked. This was a form of bread for the First People.

23

Word bank

warning
fungi
expert
fruit
reeds
stalks
Macadamia
bunya
popular
Queensland
wattle
crushed
flour
cooked
Lilly Pillies
aboriginal
grasslands
healthy
important
desert
bread

24